A Hug Just Isn't Enough

Caren Ferris

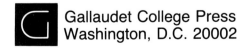
Gallaudet College Press
Washington, D.C. 20002

Published by the Gallaudet College Press
Kendall Green, Washington, D.C. 20002

Library of Congress Catalog Card
Number 80-67696

Gallaudet College is an equal opportunity employer/educational institution. Programs and services offered by Gallaudet College receive substantial financial support from the Department of Education.

ISBN 0-913580-62-7

Acknowledgements

I wish to express my appreciation to the families who contributed to this book for sharing themselves and their feelings so others could benefit from their experiences.

I am also grateful to the school personnel who permitted me to photograph the children in their programs.

And I thank my friends who gave me support and valuable feedback as I worked on this book.

Contents

Preface

Within this book a group of parents share some of the experiences they had as they made decisions to meet the needs of their young, hearing impaired children. Each child is an individual with personal needs and personal resources. Every family situation is unique. A decision that successfully meets one child's needs may not be appropriate or the best course of action for another child.

Parents make decisions for their child based on what they know about the child and what they know about available assistance. They modify their attitudes and decisions as they, the parents, grow and learn more about their child, learn more about the impact of the child's hearing loss, and learn more about external resources.

1

Goals Parents Have for Their Deaf Children

Most of the interviewed parents expressed their hopes that their deaf children would be happy, independent, and able to make their own decisions. Along with these ideas, the parents expressed their desires that their children:

—develop their individual talents and interests
—obtain a good education, including college
—acquire a job fitting to their ability
—contribute to society
—fall in love, marry, and raise their own families

The parents had different expectations with regard to whether their deaf children would live in a deaf environment, hearing environment, or both.

"It's Eric's choice to be what he wants. I'm not going to tell him what to do with his life."

"I hope Adrienne will be able to remain comfortable in the mainstream of life. I hope she will be able to accept her deafness and make the necessary adjustments to participate in the hearing world."
(hearing parent)

"We want Terry to grow up and be independent, to make his own way in the world, to get a job, to get married if he wants, to go to college, to be happy at what he chooses."

"We hope Heather develops her academic, artistic, and athletic abilities."

"Kevin will have to choose himself if he is going to spend his life with deaf people, hearing people, or both." (hearing parent)

"I'm hearing. I want my children to live in a hearing world. There are more hearing people than there are deaf people. I feel if Stacie and Bobbi Sue marry hearing boys, it would be easier for them in a hearing world." (hearing parent)

"Troy and Eric will probably gravitate toward a deaf community." (hearing parent)

"We want Charlie to get a good job. It is critical that he go to college. He has intellectual ability."

"I want Teddy to be happy. I don't want him to be a signing adult. I would like Teddy to marry a hearing girl and have hearing children."
(hearing parent)

"I don't have the goal for my children to be in the hearing world. I know from my experience of trying to attend school in a hearing environment how frustrating it can be."
(deaf parent)

"Troy's future will depend on his aptitude and interests.
"I just hope that he achieves the proper preparation for living independently."

"I don't want Scott to be dependent on signs. He must realize there is a hearing world."
(hearing parent)

"Kathy will marry a boy who is deaf. There is nothing wrong with that."
(hearing parent)

"I imagine if George continues to attend the school for the deaf, when he is old enough to fall in love, it will be with one of his deaf classmates."
(hearing parent)

"I hope Stanley goes to college. I'd like him to be good in sports, too."

"We would like Edna to help other people, to become a good citizen."

"We would like Tina to go to Gallaudet College. We want her to become self-sufficient, self-supportive, and able to make her own decisions."

2

Reactions to Deafness by Hearing Parents

After first learning of their child's deafness, it is common for hearing parents to experience a strong emotional reaction. They deny the deafness of their child. They deny the condition of deafness:

—its permanence

—the reality of the impact deafness will have on their child's communication and socialization

Hearing parents usually experience feelings of sadness, disappointment, hurt, guilt, embarrassment, shame, blame, anger, bewilderment, and the feeling of being alone and isolated from the rest of the world.

These strong feelings can interfere and distort the parents' perceptions of their children and their understanding of all the advice and information that is suddenly thrust upon them.

Family tension can occur when the mother and father are at different stages at this time of emotional adjustment. Also, the child learns to manipulate his parent's feelings which adds to the strain.

Denial: Denying the Child is Deaf

"Accepting the fact that my daughter is deaf has been very hard, especially since she had normal hearing until she had the meningitis. In the beginning, I wouldn't even use the word 'deaf.' Instead, I referred to her as 'hearing impaired.' But Adrienne's audiograms show a profound hearing loss."

"We still hope Kevin will get his hearing back. Our audiologist says that the hairs are singed, and, as long as the roots aren't burned out, they have a chance to grow back. We think Kevin might be getting his hearing back now. He says, 'Mamamamamama.' And, he acts like our other boys did when they were his age."

"We prolonged it more than we should have. When Billy was nine months old, he didn't respond to his name. He slept through noises. When he didn't start talking, our relatives said it was his personality, that he was bullheaded. Finally, when Billy was a year old, we started going to doctors and clinics. We refused to accept their diagnoses."

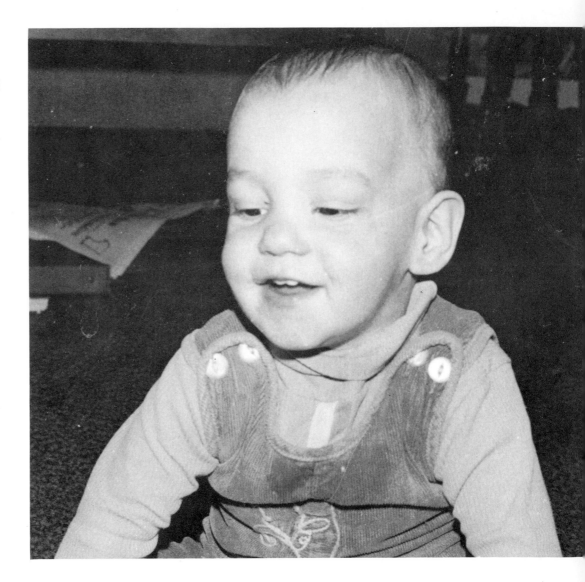

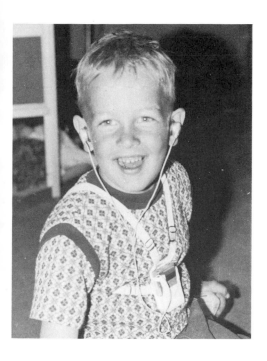

"What made it worse for us was that Charlie had some fluid in his middle ear. So, for the months while the fluid was draining, we continued to hope that was the only problem. But, his hearing loss remained the same, profound."

"I suspected Tim was deaf when he was a few weeks old. He didn't respond like his sister did when she was a baby. But everyone says no two babies are alike. I didn't admit my suspicion or mention it to my husband until Tim was a year old. My husband's response was that I was looking for trouble and was being self-conscious about the deafness already in our family."

"It was a shock to be told what we had suspected was true. Tina was deaf. We kept hoping it was anything else, tonsils, excess ear wax, anything."

Denial: Denying the Condition of Deafness

"I never give up hoping that someday, someone will develop something so Charlie will be able to hear. Maybe there will be some technological device to implant in his ear."

"I don't like the signs. I hope Scott will hear and talk . . . . Scott will talk."

"I hope Eric will be able to talk. I know it won't be as good as the other kids', but just enough so he can get by and communicate with them."

"As Sandy gets older, I think she will hear better."

"We tried acupuncture to cure Billy's deafness. That was a physically and emotionally painful experience for us all."

"If Billy doesn't hear, I pray that he will speak well enough to get along in life."

"If they can transplant a heart, why not an ear? I doubt we'll see it in our time. There could be a breakthrough at any time. It would be a miracle . . . but a possibility."
(Terry's father)

"I believe Junior will be able to hear. He's not going to be deaf for the rest of his life."

"I don't believe in miracles, except maybe, when Teddy gets older, there will be some kind of surgical development. We did go to an acupuncturist. He had the sense to tell us Teddy was too young."

Sadness

"When I hear a pretty song; this feeling comes that I want Terry to hear the music, to hear the birds, to hear a baby cry. I feel he's missing this, and I feel sorry for him. Then, I see how happy Terry is. In most everything he does, Terry seems happy. If he doesn't know these sounds, he really doesn't know what he is missing.

"When they first told me Terry was deaf, I started crying. I thought of his future and that he would never be able to work, to get married, to live an independent life. Later, I realized my feelings would reflect off Terry. I feel he will make out all right now."

"I feel sad that either one of our boys is deaf. When Troy came along, it never entered my mind that he would be deaf, too. We just felt so sad when we realized Troy was not responding to sound."

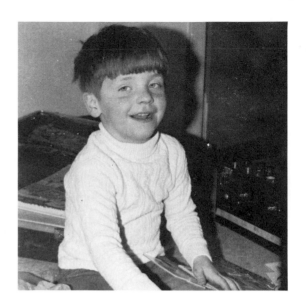

"I feel sorry for Stacie and Bobbi Sue when all the kids in the neighborhood are playing a game, and they are left out because they can't communicate. But I don't let them know I feel bad."

"When I first found out about Heather's hearing loss, I cried all the way home. I had suspected there was a hearing problem, but it was a shock to find out how bad it was. Now, I think she will do all right in spite of it."

Disappointment and Hurt

"The hardest thing for me to accept was that neither Eric nor Troy would achieve the goal I had planned for a son. I wanted my son to succeed where I was not able to. I wanted to go to military school and be a military pilot. I had hoped one of my sons would achieve this."

"I was hurt in the beginning and didn't know what to do. It was hard for Billy's father. Billy is his only son. He, like I first did, crawled into a shell."

"Sometimes it hurts. The other night Tina's grandmother told us how she talks to her other granddaughter on the telephone now. I just felt so bad."

Guilt

"Billy and his deafness put a lot of stress on our family. Things just didn't go right. I gave all my time to Billy. I was so upset I'd wake up with tremendous headaches. I was frustrated. I felt like I was at the end of my rope, on the verge of a nervous breakdown.

"I'm learning that I can get out and do more, leave the house without feeling guilty. I've started to play tennis, have lunch with friends, find my own world, find me. And, when I come home, I find I'm in better spirits with Billy because of it."

"At first I thought Junior's deafness was my fault. Now, I realize his deafness is something I can't control."

"For a long time, I was pre-occupied with the cause of Charlie's deafness. I was convinced that I didn't want any more children. Since, we didn't know what caused Charlie's deafness, I was afraid that another baby could have a handicap worse than deafness."

Embarrassment and Shame

"His father never took him anywhere."

"His father made no effort to communicate with him."

"His father pushed him aside and spent more time with our hearing child."

"George's mother used to dress George up to take him out. She would take his hearing aids off. I told her, 'Don't ever try to hide his hearing aids or the fact that George is deaf. Accept him. There is nothing to be ashamed of.' "
(George's grandmother)

"Fathers of handicapped children tend to be ashamed of the child and jealous of the attention the child gets. There's nothing to be ashamed of. Both parents should be involved with the child."
(Miki's father)

"Some people think it's a sin when a child is born deaf. Then the child feels un-wanted. Don't shut your deaf child out of your life. I know because we have a deaf child."
(Eric's mother)

"Sometimes I'm embar-rassed in a shopping mall around a lot of people. I don't put Charlie's hearing aid on him."

Blame

"The deafness aggravated the family situation. Everything wrong was my fault. Of course, that included our child being deaf. I was blamed for his deafness." (divorced parent)

"Even though we knew when we were married that there was deafness in the family, we planned on having children. The possibility of having a deaf child was always in the back of my mind. But you don't really expect it to happen to you. No matter whose side of the family the deafness is on, you shouldn't blame anyone." (Tim's Mother)

Bewilderment

"Why does this happen to me? I tried to accept my first son's deafness. Can I accept it with Troy, too? Did we really have a problem or were we creating it ourselves? I didn't want to think about it."

"We just didn't understand the whole thing, Kathy Ann and her becoming deaf."

"When I see all the deaf children, I just wonder, 'Why?' "

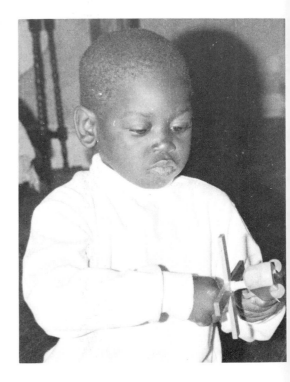

"I've never been around deaf people before. At first, I said I couldn't understand them, but each day I am learning more how to cope with Junior."

Aloneness

"At first, I felt I was in this situation all by myself. I felt better when I learned I wasn't alone. Learning about educational programs for deaf children helped. Knowing that George wouldn't have to just sit home and be deaf made me feel better."

"Now I'm aware that I'm not the only father who has a deaf daughter."
(Adrienne's father)

Sources of Support and Direction

"My husband and I have tried to help each other."

"Talking with professionals has helped."

"The biggest help for us has been meeting and talking with deaf people."

"Self determination. My strength came from my desire to help my child."

"Through prayer, God has given me strength to accept this problem."

"I learned a lot from talking with other parents of deaf children."

"Seeing my child's progress and accomplishments has made me feel better."

3

Parental Acceptance

The role of parent requires constant decision making. Parents make decisions that effect their child's whole life. For a parent to make good decisions, he must know his child and he must accept him. Parents of a hearing impaired child need to comprehend what it is to be deaf and then accept the concept of deafness within their child.

The child's responses to his parents' decisions serve as the best guide and provide the most reliable feedback to the parents. When there is an honest understanding of the hearing loss and an acceptance of the child, parents can more clearly see their child's needs and his progress.

As hearing parents learn more about deafness, their initial emotional response subsides. In turn, as their emotional tension is reduced, parents are better able to understand and accept the idea of deafness.

Acceptance: From Deaf Parents

"When Saralee was one week old and she didn't show any response to noise, we knew she was hearing impaired. We didn't have any hysterical reaction. It gives us the greatest challenge to raise Saralee as a fine, intelligent girl. Saralee gives us much joy. She inspires us. Saralee can accomplish as much as and more than a normally hearing child."

"I think it is wonderful to have deaf children. We are happy that both our children are deaf. It makes our family close."
(Robin's parents)

Acceptance: From Hearing Parents

"There's not one thing wrong with Chrissy or her sisters. They function just as normally as you or I do. When people say, 'Why did you have all those children?' I get really irritated. To me, my daughters are intelligent, beautiful, and full of love. I tell those people, 'I accept them as my children. I plan to have more children. We couldn't be prouder.' "

"It's a great feeling for me to see Billy do so many normal things. I don't look at him as handicapped anymore. Now, when I see other handicapped people, I make an effort to go up and talk to them."

"Bobbi and Stacie aren't any different except we use signs as we talk, and we have to run after them instead of hollering to them."

"I see other handicapped people in a worse condition, and I feel good about all that Junior can do. I have a lot to be thankful for."

"You get over your emotions so you can help your child. "Because we have a good feeling about Charlie's deafness, he has a good feeling about it. We try to create an environment where Charlie doesn't think deafness is a special thing."

"After learning Tim really was deaf, the next step was to find out how to help him, not to sit and brood over it. "I look at Timmy, and he is so happy. "Someday Tim is going to hear, whether it be here or in Heaven."

"Whether Eric is deaf or not, we love him a whole lot. It's not his fault he was born deaf."

"With the sickness Terry had, his deafness was easier to accept. We are fortunate that there is nothing else wrong, and that Terry is doing as well as he is. "We can tell you we have accepted Terry's deafness, but in the back of our minds, we want Terry to be a hearing boy."

"Kevin may be deaf, but he is normal in every other way. He gets his cuts and bruises like any kid. He can drive you crazy like any kid. He can love you like any kid."

23

4

Common Frustrations

As parents seek professional services, they often encounter frustrating experiences such as professionals inexperienced with pre-school aged deaf children, a lack of information, misinformation, conflicting information, poor advice, the "run-around," a lack of services, and financial exploitation.

Frustration: Inexperienced Professionals and Lack of Information

"My pediatrician told me that neither one of the boys is deaf and that I was just looking for something to be wrong with them."
(Eric and Troy's mother)

"When Robin went to have his hearing tested for a new hearing aid, they didn't believe him when he didn't respond to the sounds. Robin was confused, yet they kept trying to make him respond."

"When Scott was a little over two years old, he just stopped talking. The doctor said nothing was wrong. This doctor still does not acknowledge the fact that Scott has a hearing loss."

"I was suspicious of a hearing problem when Heather was 9 months old. It wasn't confirmed until she was over three years old. My pediatrician kept telling me Heather was too young to identify a hearing loss."

"Where Tim was tested, they didn't take the time to make friends with him. They just rushed us from one doctor to another. When Tim started to cry, they told me my child wouldn't cooperate."

"There is no place to get information about anything: schools, county services, parent instruction . . . We damn near begged people to tell us information. We tried the public library, the Board of Education, the Health Department. We ran up against a brick wall.

"It would be easier on the parent and on the child if we knew what to be prepared for. The first week we learned Miki had a hearing loss, we stopped talking to her. We figured why bother. Miki couldn't understand the change in us.

"There should be more education given to parents on the care and problems that go along with the hearing aid: the feedback, getting a good earmold fit, etc. With Miki, we found this out by trial and error."

"There I was with Scott, a three year old deaf child. And I didn't know what to do. 'Put him in a school,' they said. 'Get all the help you can. Get speech therapy.' But no one told me where to get help."

"When I first received Tim's hearing aid, no one told me how high to set it. After one year, the audiologist told me I had it turned down too low. "I didn't know the whistling sound came from ill-fitting earmolds."

Frustration: Misinformation and Poor Advice

"One audiologist led me to believe Eric was hard of hearing and that he should go to public school. I was advised to have nothing to do with the school for the deaf. I knew that a child who could only say, 'mama,' 'papa,' and 'hi,' was not ready for first grade in public school.

"We paid another professional $125 to tell us that both Eric and Troy were deaf and that the best thing for us to do was to put them in a school across the country, visit them once a year, and start living our own life."

"I was finally sent to an Ear-Nose-Throat specialist. He recommended that Heather not have a hearing test until she was at least four years old. He told me they condition the children to the sounds with electrical shocks. I knew better than that."

Frustration: Conflicting Information

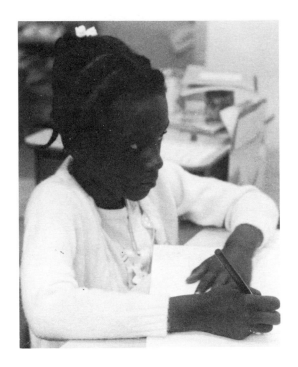

"Unfortunately, there is a stupid fight going on among the professionals. Some advocate an oral approach to communication. Others support the total approach. Both sides are deeply biased, and I suspect neither knows what the other is doing. The losers are the children. We parents are caught in the middle. We have to decide about our child's future and his education."
(Adrienne's mother)

"I feel like I'm caught in the middle.
    Someone says I should send Julie and Kristy to the school for the deaf.
    Someone else says they should stay in public school.
    Someone says we should use signs.
    Someone else says signs are bad.
All parents want to do what's best for their children. The problem is knowing what is best."

Frustration: The "Run-around"

"I felt that the people who tested Miki weren't telling me what I wanted to know. They tended to treat me as if I wouldn't understand what they were talking about, like I was dumb. I would have liked to have been told the facts and alternatives from the beginning, so I could make future plans and adjust to the problem. They didn't want to commit themselves. They kept asking me if I thought Miki had a hearing loss. If I didn't, I wouldn't have come there in the first place. They gave her an EEG test. When I asked about the results, they said the results were inconclusive. Why, then, did they bother to give the test? You feel like they are running you from one place to another without getting any information."

"Genetic counseling was a disappointment. They told us there was a probability that our next child would be deaf, too, but they couldn't say for sure. We walked away not knowing anymore than when we came."
(Stacie and Bobbi Sue's parents)

Frustration: Lack of Services

"I wish there were closer facilities. My father had to take off from work to get Sandy's hearing aid. We have to go back because the earmolds don't fit. It's a six hour drive."

"There aren't facilities in our area for servicing Tim's hearing aid. I have to run around for new molds, new batteries, and for repair service."

Frustration: Financial Exploitation

"We have to buy a new hearing aid for Charlie every five years. We could have used some financial help, especially when we were younger and just starting out. When the school audiologist recommended Charlie get a new hearing aid, we waited until his old aid completely died. Seven hundred dollars is a lot of money. I think the cost of hearing aids is a rip-off."

"We have never received any help for the cost of hearing tests, hearing aids, etc. We've had to deny ourselves things. We've paid $2900 for hearing aids. Each trip for a hearing evaluation costs $35-40. Troy has chewed through 3 or 4 sets of earmolds at $20 each."

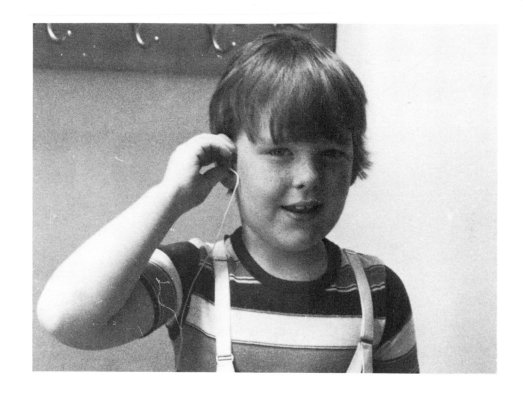

"The hearing aid dealers in our area take advantage of the situation. When we brought Heather's aid in for repair, we were charged $40. After waiting a month for it, it still wasn't fixed right. We learned to go to professionals who can recommend choices. The variation in price is incredible. We paid $685 for Heather's hearing aid. The local dealer would have charged $1500."

5

Meeting the Deaf Child's Need for Family Life

A primary need for every child is for him to feel that he belongs to his family. The deaf child learns to identify himself as a family member by actively joining the everyday family routine, by actively participating in the family responsibility, and by actively sharing in the family recreation.

All children need to learn discipline and self-control, to respect limits, and to accept responsibility. It is sometimes more difficult for hearing parents to discipline their deaf child because:

—The parent has not yet learned to cope with his feelings, and, consequently, does not feel comfortable putting demands on his child.

—The effort to communicate is too hard for the parent.

A lack of discipline affects the whole family structure as well as the individual deaf child. The family can become tyrannized by the spoiled, handicapped child. Tension occurs when hearing brothers and sisters are expected to follow a different set of rules as their deaf sibling follows. The deaf child needs to be treated as an equal member of his family, and not as a guest with special privileges.

Children need the opportunity to personally experience the world in which they live. Overprotection inhibits a child's growth. It is the family who provides the child with opportunities to learn through exploration and play.

The Deaf Child as a Family Participant

"We do a lot together. We seldom go out without Heather. We play tennis, play miniature golf, roller skate, ice skate, canoe, bike, and camp together."

"Junior sees me doing things, and he wants to copy. When I was learning to play the piccolo, he wanted to play, too. So I bought toy ones for him and his sister. We used to practice, the three of us together, making music. It was fun."

"I try to let George be a part of our everyday living. I don't want him to be left out or feel different.

"I take George to church because the family goes to church. George sits with the other children and wears his choir robe. When the children sing, George claps his hands and beats a tambourine. For the Christmas play, I taught George to sign, 'Jesus was born on Christmas Day.' Everyone thought he was wonderful.

"We have a happy family life. George's handicap has not made any difference to our family."

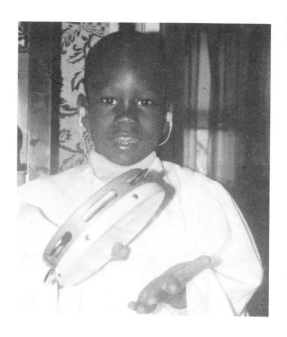

"Sandy likes to be helpful. She makes her bed, dusts, and does the dishes."

"Tim works outside with his daddy a lot. He drives the tractor, prepares the ground for planting, carries hay to the cows, cleans the barn, mows the grass, cleans the milk machines, tills the family garden. Inside, Tim helps with the vacuuming and likes to help bake bread."

"Tina helps me with Tony. She gets his diaper, picks up his toys, and plays with him."

"Miki helped when we put up new wallpaper. We include Miki in whatever we are doing. Yet, we don't turn our life around for her.

"We teach Miki safety. We have fire drills. We teach her how to cross the street and ride her bike carefully."

"Kathy Ann loves to bake pies with me. We all work in the garden together. We take the kids bowling. They seem to like to play house and ride their bikes best."

35

Discipline

"There is nothing special about Kathy Ann. She is like the other kids. I try not to treat her special. Believe me, it's hard to do. I sometimes catch myself being easier with her than with the other kids."

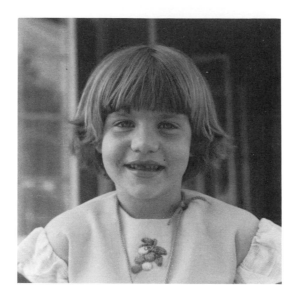

"It takes more of an effort to discipline a child than it takes to be permissive. This is especially true for a deaf child because of the communication problem. Being permissive is just an easy way out, a short cut." (Teddy's father)

"I explain to my children that when we punish them it is because we love them and want them to grow up honest and truthful.
"Sometimes, the girls try to take advantage of their deafness. They ignore us or pretend they don't understand what we are telling them to do. But we know they understand what is going on and don't let them get away with that trick." (Chrissy's mother)

"The other night in the store, Troy wanted a candy bar. I told him he couldn't have it because he had been bad earlier. A lady who had been watching me came up and said, 'Poor little boy. He can't hear. I'll buy him the candy bar.' It would have been easier to just get Troy the candy, but that's not my responsibility as a parent."

"When Kevin needs love, we give him love. When he needs a spanking, we give him one."

"I treat Adrienne as if she were a normally hearing child. As long as she understands, she is accountable for her behavior."

"Miki will sometimes try to use her hearing loss. She'll say, 'I don't understand you. I'm a little bit hard of hearing, you know.' When she wants her way, she turns off her hearing aids. We are not afraid to discipline Miki. We don't make excuses for her."

Learning Through Play

"Bobbi Sue likes to play with her dolls, to feed them, to dress them. She loves her Baby-Alive doll that she feeds and then it messes in its diaper. All Bobbi's allowance goes for buying Pampers for that doll."

"Scott is inquisitive. He has to satisfy his curiosity. He finds things around the house to take apart so he can see how they work."

"We found out Heather can do what hearing children do.
"Heather has received recognition for her art work. Her design was selected for Easter Seals. She entered her nutrition poster in a county wide contest and won first prize.
"Heather likes to cook, hook rugs, and do needlework.
"She is in a Brownie Troop.
"Heather takes tap dancing, ballet, and gymnastic lessons. Her school has asked her to join their gymnastics team.
"Heather has a stamp collection."
"Heather enjoys doing academically creative things. She has written her own book of poetry:"

What is Blue?
Blue is the sky
And the sky's cry.
The lake
You'll never have to rake.

You
You is not me,
It couldn't be.
If I were you,
Nothing would do.

Me
Me is only me.
I'm happy as can be.
You see,
Nobody is going to be me.

"We let Billy be creative with tools. He does his own thing. He gets dirty, greasy, muddy. Billy made the roof to his tree house."

6

Meeting the Deaf Child's Need for Communication

Deafness creates a serious communication problem. Deafness handicaps:
- —a child's ability to acquire English language
- —a child's ability to understand oral communication
- —a child's ability to express himself orally

In our culture, knowledge of the English language is necessary for communication, for the giving and receiving of information. Knowledge of the English sentence structure and English grammar is a prerequisite for successfully reading and writing in English. The acquisition of English is a difficult, yet achievable goal for deaf children. It is a necessary condition for the deaf person to function comfortably and successfully in our total culture.

Parents decide how to communicate with their deaf child:
- —by using English language, American Sign Language, no formal language system, or a combination
- —by using the aural approach, the oral approach, the manual approach, the total approach, or a combination.

Communication

"We feel any means of communication is worthwhile: signs, gestures, any form of communication. We want to communicate with our son.
"Without communication, you don't have anything.
"Communication is a two-way street."

"We use total communication with Terry. We sign and talk in English. Terry signs and uses some voice back. We feel total communication is right. We will continue to use it as long as Terry needs it."

"We learned from deaf adults that if we didn't learn to communicate with our children by the time they were 12 years old, we never would. A lot of deaf people we met resent their hearing parents because their parents never bothered to communicate with them. We didn't want that for our family.
"Deaf people helped us realize the need to use total communication all the time in Roger and Tommy's presence, and not just when we talk directly to them. Children learn more by participating in conversations. So, everything we say in front of the boys we sign. If we don't sign it, we don't say it.
"When you hear your deaf child say a word, you think maybe he doesn't need signs. But you have to be careful not to confuse speech ability with language."

"A deaf child needs a total communication, signed English exposure to know what is going on.

"Before we started using total communication, we had trouble understanding what Roger was telling us. When he couldn't succeed in communicating his idea after two or three tries, he just gave up and turned away. That scared us.

"Roger and Tom have internalized the basic English language structure. They frequently choose to communicate orally. When there is a misunderstanding, they use manual skills for clarification.

"It can be a burden to sign everything. Signing is hard for us. It's not our natural form of communication. We didn't learn signs when we were little. But we want Roger and Tom to learn as much as they can. They are always learning. So, we continue to use signed English and total communication with them.

"It's worth the effort if you don't want your child to be left out of his family."

"We use the aural/oral method to communicate with Teddy. He listens and lip-reads our verbal communication. Teddy uses his voice and gestures to communicate to us.

"We weighed the aural/oral method and the total communication method. Everyone should have a shot at oralism. You can always fall back on total communication.

"We have seen deaf children learn aurally without using any visual cues.

"We've recently changed to a private therapist who emphasizes the development of Teddy's listening skills. Teddy goes to therapy four hours a week at $15 an hour. We usually have an hour's worth of homework a night.

"We cover our mouths so Teddy won't rely on lipreading. It's a hard decision to cover your mouth. We want Teddy to become a listener and then use oral methods.

"Right now, Teddy is behind in his language development. Most authorities say there is a critical period during which children acquire language. We are in a frustrated state. Teddy is starting to use connected language. That gives us hope to continue the oral approach. It's getting late. It's hard to decide. We don't want Teddy to lose out with academics. We don't want him to become frustrated. We will watch Teddy's progress closely. If he is not acquiring language, we will switch to total communication before too much time goes by."

"Billy used to pull at me and cry. We didn't know what he wanted. That was hard on us. The signs have helped. Billy can now communicate to us what he wants.

"I used to be embarrassed to take Billy into a store. He would holler if he didn't get what he wanted. Everyone would stare. Now, we enjoy shopping together. Our improved communication has made the difference. I sign the food name and fingerspell the brand. Billy brings the food to the cart."
(Billy's mother)

"I finally faced up to the problem. I needed to use sign language to communicate with Billy. He was starting to get upset when he couldn't get his idea across to me. He stopped trying. My son started to lose interest in me. Now, Billy sees me as wanting to communicate. My advice to fathers is to learn to sign as early as you can. Get involved."
(Billy's father)

"We communicate orally with Miki now. Miki would not be where she is now without signs. Many people told us that if Miki learned signs too young, she would depend on them, and it would interfere with her speech development. Using signs has helped Miki tremendously. We still use signs when she is having a problem understanding or when her hearing aids are not working."

"The signs have helped with the discipline. Now, we can sign to Kathy Ann, and she understands what we are telling her."

"I question whether signs aren't used instead of voice simply because it's easier."
(Adrienne's mother)

"The fear I had was if Eric and Troy learned to talk on their hands, they wouldn't learn to use their voices."

"Kathy Ann gets disgusted at our not being able to sign."

"I was against using signs with Heather in the beginning. I thought she would stop talking. But, using signs was a definite stage to go through. There was a time when her frustration was bad. We didn't understand each other. Using signs has also helped Heather increase her vocabulary, acquire sentence structure, and achieve language. Her speech and lipreading skills have continued to improve. "Heather announced to us one day that she didn't want to use signs anymore. So, we stopped. Heather no longer needed them."

"Initially, I refused to learn signs. It has been easier for Adrienne and me since I accepted the need for signs. When I first signed a whole sentence to Adrienne, 'We are going to buy shoes,' she was really proud. Adrienne looked at me as if to say, 'Why haven't you signed like this before?' Our communication has been much better. I realize now that using signs is the best way to communicate."
(Adrienne's father)

"I can remember the feeling of accomplishment when Tim first signed back to me. He said, 'Kitty eat.'"

"We have been using total communication, mostly manual communication, with Saralee since her birth. When she was six months old, she said her first word in sign, 'dog.'"

"Hearing parents shouldn't expect their deaf children to communicate as hearing children. Trying to make the deaf child oral furthers his handicap."
(Stacie and Bobbi Sue's mother)

"What scared us was whether Charlie would be able to communicate with other people. We knew we would be able to communicate with him."

"Stanley learned signs fast. He likes to take his books to bed with him at night and ask us what the pictures are. When we show him the signs, Stanley copies them. Stanley is always asking us for the signs of things he sees."

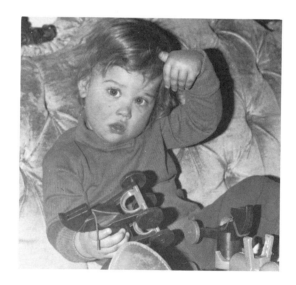

"We've been using total communication with Charlie since he was 13 months old. In the beginning, Charlie would tell us one thing or bits and pieces of an idea. Then, he started to tell us complete thoughts. He would get all excited when he told us things. After a few years, he began to understand when we told him about future events. You have to be patient and stick with the signing. The language will come.
"Now, Charlie demands to know what we are saying when we talk without signing."

"I fail to understand why the total communication community tends to isolate themselves. This is a hearing world, and sign language is only useful when there is someone else who knows signs. While I see the need for sign language to explan the world and its workings to deaf people, I can't see why they want to segregate themselves."
(Adrienne's mother)

Learning to Sign

"We were so upset that we couldn't learn signs. I wanted my children to talk. I really fought the signs.
"I've come a long way with signing, and I have a long way to go.
"I don't know as many signs as I should. There's not much opportunity to use signs when the boys are away at school all week.
"Eric and Troy teach us more signs than we ever learned at sign classes. We tell them that they are our teachers."
"The signing is becoming easier all the time."

"I didn't want to learn signs. It was such a nuisance. But I did it. My husband and I both went to sign classes." (Charlie's mother)

"I wanted signs all at once, right away. But it doesn't work that way. I didn't think I would ever learn the signs." (Stacy's mother)

"Kathy Ann seems to understand more signs than she is expressing."

"Since Edna is our youngest child, she has observed her brother and sisters' signed communication. Edna learned to sign easily."

"Before Troy went to school, Eric taught him the signs he was learning at school. Eric took Troy's fingers and helped him form the signs. This helped Troy."

"I'm afraid to sign, afraid I'll do it wrong. I feel so clumsy." (Kenny's mother)

"The signs are hard to learn."

"I still want to learn signs better."

Different Signs for the Same Word

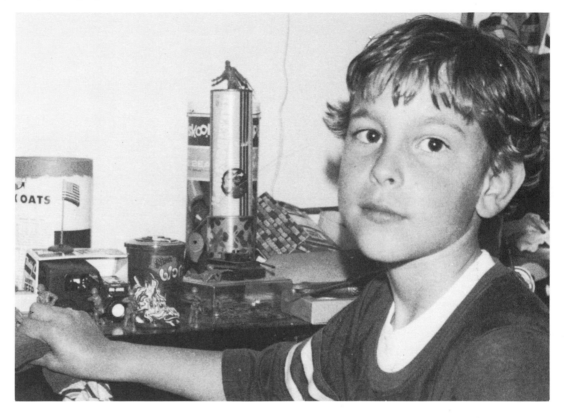

"When we were first learning signs, it was frustrating the way the signs kept changing. We decided to use what we liked. It's a mixture. We are not rigid about which sign to use. I use whatever sign comes to mind. I can use a completely wrong sign, and Charlie still understands me. He used to correct me, but he has stopped that. The good thing is that the children can adapt. Charlie knows different signs for the same word."

"I'm disappointed that they keep inventing new signs. Robin understands that I use old signs, and that there is nothing wrong with the old signs. Sometimes he tells me I'm using the wrong sign. I tell Robin he can use whatever he wants and that I'm using the old signs."

"I just ignored the people who told me I was using the wrong sign. It really doesn't matter which sign you use as long as your child understands the word."
(Tom and Roger's father)

"Adrienne corrects me if I'm not using the sign she is used to. I change over to the sign she knows."

"The children don't worry about which sign we adults use. Billy uses old and new signs for the same word."

"Saralee's pre-school aged sisters go to a different school. They sometimes use different signs. We use both at home."

"Miki knows what I mean regardless of which sign I use."

Signed English, American Sign Language

"We didn't use signs until Stacie was three years old. Bobbi Sue has been exposed to signed English since her birth. We see a big difference between our girls' sentence structure and language. Using signed English from the time you know your child is deaf really helps him."

"When we sign to Eric and Troy, it's more like signs put together than signed English."

"I mostly sign in sentences to Stacy. When I'm busy, I don't always put the endings on."

"Signing in English is easy for me. But I'm not sure it's easy for deaf people. I don't know if we hearing people are right to discriminate and insist the deaf learn our language. Deaf people are able to get their message across with very few words using ASL."
(Tim's mother)

"We use ASL or signed English depending on what Robin is using. We answer back in whatever language he uses to talk to us."

"I sign and talk to my daughters using both ASL and signed English. Because my mother and father are deaf, I was raised using ASL. Sometimes, it's hard to remember to use correct English."
(Chrissy's mother)

Fingerspelling

"I went to a school for the deaf where we always finger spelled and never used signs. I believe deaf children should learn to fingerspell more. It would improve their spelling ability.

"I encourage Robin to fingerspell. He is motivated to learn spelling because he wants to talk on our TTY to his friend Saralee. Robin was frustrated when she called him, and he couldn't spell out his message to her."

"I use fingerspelling as part of the total communication I use with Adrienne. If I don't know the sign for a word, I always fingerspell it so Adrienne knows there is a name for the word. Also, I spell the names of specific items instead of using a general sign. For example, I spell out the different kinds of candy names instead of just signing them all as candy. This way, Adrienne learns so much more."

Hearing Aids

"We don't force Tim to wear his hearing aid. The cords are always getting in his way when he plays."

"Terry hasn't been wearing his aids much lately. He has had several ear infections, and he just had his adenoids removed."

"Heather puts her hearing aids on first thing every morning."

"Miki doesn't feel dressed unless she has her hearing aids in."

"George wears his hearing aid all the time. At first, he cried and pulled it off. He didn't want me to put it on. I just kept putting it on every day until he got used to it. Now, he puts it on himself."

"Teddy rejected his hearing aid for three years before he would wear it. He adjusts it himself now."

"If children don't have much hearing or are profoundly deaf, I don't think they should use a hearing aid. Robin refuses to wear his. We don't force him."

"We have one rule about hearing aids at home: Troy and Eric must wear their hearing aids when they are riding their bikes."

"Edna wants a hearing aid. They cost too much money. They require too much care."

"We bought Bobbi and Stacie post-aural aids because they wanted to be like the other kids at school. We hoped they would wear their hearing aids more if they had the same style as the other kids. But, they still choose not to wear their hearing aids at home. They just don't get that much benefit from wearing them. We are concerned that at school they don't see many deaf adults wearing hearing aids. Also, when they stayed in the dorm, the dorm counselors had the children take their aids off after school."

"Even with her hearing aids, Kathy Ann doesn't understand some things being said."

Speech

"I wish Terry could speak more. He really tries to say 'mama.' Terry knows people use their mouths to carry meaning. I'd like to hear Terry speak, but if he doesn't, it won't upset me. I know that if I concentrated too much on his not being able to speak, it would interfere with our relationship."

"Junior wants to talk. Everyone he is around talks. He tries so hard. It just hurts me so badly when he fumbles around and can't say the words."

"Teddy has had enough oral background to tell us things. Instead, he just points and says, 'uh.' He's not producing speech. I'm dissatisfied with the quality of his production and the rate of words."

"Sometimes I can't understand Chrissy unless she uses her voice. It's not so much her voice as my lipreading her mouth movements that helps."

"I never expected Charlie's speech to be as good as it is. It really is intelligible. We haven't found the signs to impede his speech. Charlie tries to speak as long as he wears his hearing aid."

"At first, we couldn't even find a speech therapist who would work with a deaf child. Now, Heather's speech is so good that her therapist feels he has gone as far as he can with her. We continue to work with her continuously ourselves."

"When the children are little, they need all the speech work they can get. Having a deaf teacher did not help Scott's speech. I want Scott to have as much speech work as possible."

"Sandy speaks with one syllable at a time. I thought her speech would be better."

"We are disappointed with Troy's speech. There are few words we can understand, just 'mama,' 'papa,' 'hi,' 'bye,' 'boy,' and 'pizza.'"

"Eric is trying to say more and more with his voice. I make him use his voice. He can say the names of everyone at home."

"We wanted Bobbi Sue and Stacie to have more time and individual lessons for speech. This was not possible at school due to the ratio of children to the number of speech therapists. So, we decided to send the girls to private speech therapy. They go for a half hour lesson a week and bring home work that we follow through on during the week.
"We don't expect them to speak perfectly clear. But, we would like for them to be able to communicate in the hearing world. Deaf adults have advised us that even though they intensely hated speech therapy as children, the lessons proved valuable in their ability to lipread and to speak to hearing people."

"There is more clarity to Adrienne's speech now. She is saying words more than just sounds. It frequently is not clear enough for other people, but I understand most of it."

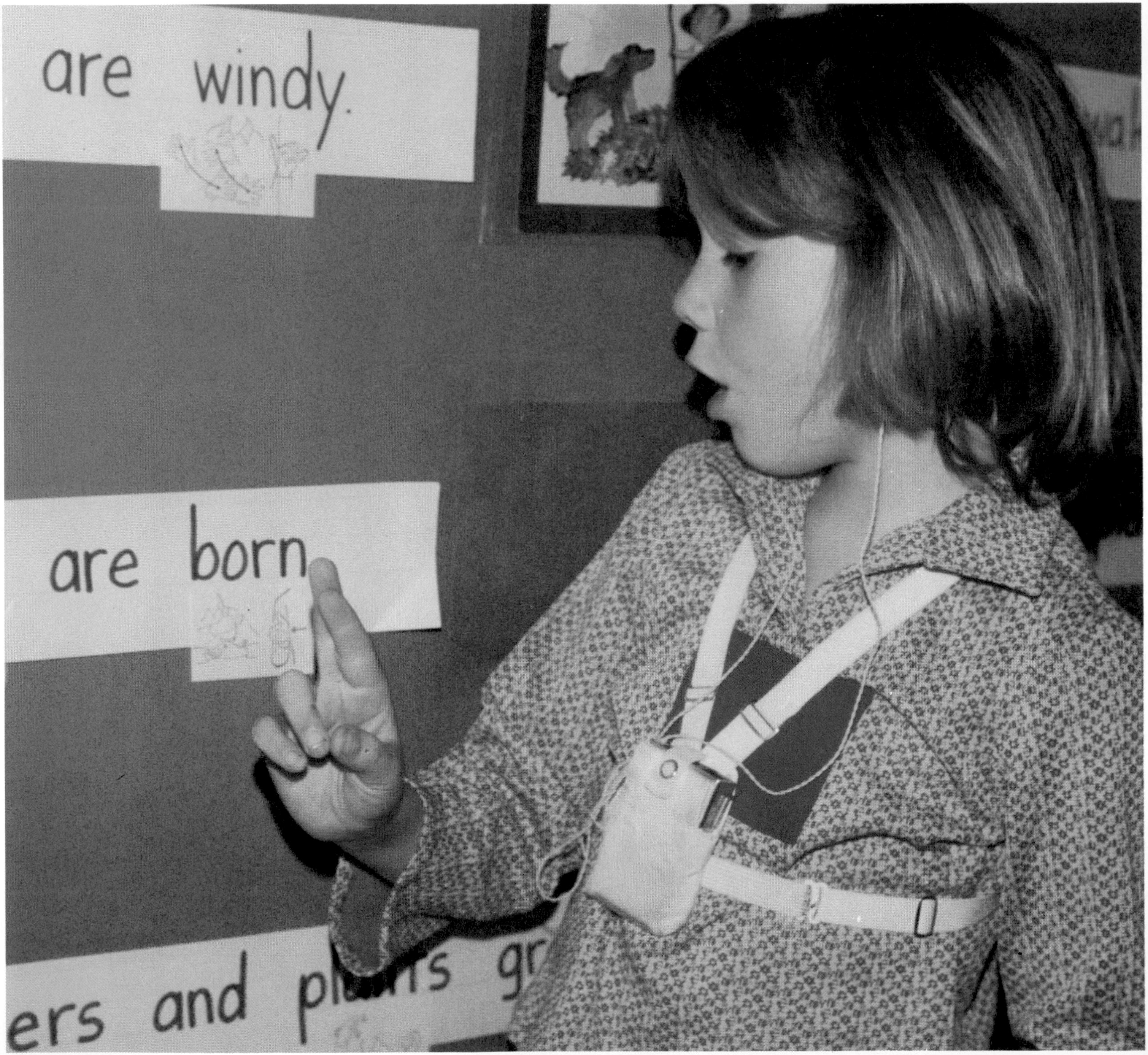
are windy.
are born
ers and plants gr

7

Meeting the Deaf Child's Need for Education

Parents decide the educational placement for their deaf children. Most deaf children need a special environment for learning. Those deaf children who do successfully mainstream in the public schools, partially or totally, need supportive services and continuous monitoring of their progress. Some considerations for selecting the environment that is going to promote the deaf child's emotional growth, social development, and academic achievement are:
  —the individual child's abilities
  —professionals trained and experienced in the areas of child development, deafness, and learning
  —peers with whom the deaf child can successfully interact
  —academic and social programming that is designed specifically for deaf children
  —materials and equipment that facilitate the program goals
Parents have choices to investigate:
  —Is the local special education program comprehensive?
  —Is the state program with a larger, homogeneous population better able to serve deaf children?
  —Should the child be a day student?
  —Should the child be residentially placed?
For any child, maximum success in learning occurs when the family and school have the same goals, work together, and support each other.

Mainstreaming

"We though we would try sending Heather to public school and see how it worked. We were concerned because the schools for the deaf are behind the public schools academically. We didn't want to send Heather away from home. And the deaf children we observed at the school for the deaf seemed to prefer to use signs. Heather is our only child. She is bright and has a high I.Q. We are committed to working with her.

"When Heather was four years old, she went ½ day to kindergarten. The next year, she repeated kindergarten and went ½ day to a special classroom for hearing impaired children. This program was discontinued because there were not enough children to justify it.

"Heather went into first grade already knowing how to read and how to add. We taught Heather how to read phonetically when she was four years old to compensate for her hearing deficiency.

"Heather loved first grade and her teacher. She came home and played school. "Heather did very well in first grade. We went right into her classroom and observed to make sure of her progress. We had a few concerns which we took to our school superintendent. He acted on them immediately.

"The only special treatment Heather receives in school is that she sits up front to better read her teacher's lips. And she is permitted to read the accompanying dialogue books when her class sees (and hears) a movie.

"For second grade, Heather has been doing advanced reading and advanced math. She participates in a special program for gifted children. Although she is functioning at the 5th grade level or higher academically, Heather selects her friends from her second grade class. Socially, Heather is popular. Occasionally, she has typical childhood tiffs with her friends.

"There may be a problem when she gets older and has more lecture type classes. We will continue to take each week, each year, each situation as it comes. "Heather is happy in school. She is capable of keeping up with her class and surpassing them academically. We are pleased with our educational decision."

"I wanted to keep Julie and Kristy home. There's not much of a homelife in a residential school. I was also concerned about the low level of education that the graduate of deaf schools achieved. I thought we'd give the local program a try and see how well the girls progressed. As long as Julie and Kristy keep progressing academically, I'm satisfied.

"Julie started kindergarten a year early and repeated it. Now, she is with her age level hearing peers for math, science, lunch, and recess.

"The rest of the school day Julie works with a resource teacher who is trained in deaf education. He uses total communication with Julie. The children work individually with the resource teacher or his aide on reading, auditory training, and on any work they don't understand from the regular class. Julie also receives speech therapy services."

"Terry has P.E., art, lunch, and recess with hearing children. Terry plays well with the hearing children. One time the P.E. teacher sent a hearing girl to get Terry for P.E. Terry didn't understand why the girl was pulling on him. So, he bit her. The teacher went to the hearing girl's class to explain that Terry didn't bite the girl out of meanness. We're not kidding ourselves. Terry doesn't have enough language to fully mainstream."

"We knew we'd send Tina to the state school for the deaf. She wouldn't get anywhere in a hearing school situation. She'd be ignored, on the bottom of the heap. I'm a teacher, and I've heard other teachers tell of children who suffered because they needed special education and their parents refused it. As a teacher, I think it might be difficult for a deaf child to receive the same education as his hearing peers in the same class."

"Kathy Ann doesn't belong in a public school. I wouldn't even consider it. Kathy Ann is a deaf child, and she belongs with deaf peers.

"Kathy Ann has accepted the school for the deaf as her school."

"I'd like to have Billy try mainstreaming in a few years. He does so well with his hearing sister and her friends. There are two worlds, a deaf world and a hearing world. I want to give Billy a chance in the hearing world, let him try."

"Tim wouldn't survive in a mainstreaming program."

"It doesn't seem fair to the child, to put him in a regular school. Deaf children need special educational help." (Kevin's mother)

"Mainstreaming in a public school would be all right if George received the same quality of education as he is receiving at the school for the deaf."

"Mainstreaming is good only if the children are ready for it. You can't just dump them into mainstreaming without first looking at each child individually." (Adrienne's mother)

"I doubt Miki could cope if she were with 25 hearing children and one teacher. When she was in the Head Start program, there were 20 kids, one teacher, and two aides. Miki still missed what was going on. Miki is progressing very well at the school for the deaf. She is more advanced in academics than her hearing peers. Miki understands what she is reading. I feel she is getting a better education than if she were in a public school. We are delighted with her progress."

Special Education

"Only where a large number of deaf children are educated together can a program provide not only age and ability grouping, but also high quality auditory equipment and a full range of curricular and extra-curricular activities, facilities, and materials designed for severely and profoundly deaf children."

David M. Denton
Superintendent
Maryland School for the Deaf

"Scott's public school kindergarten teacher said he wasn't ready for first grade. Scott isn't slow. Mentally, he was ready for school. It was the language that was holding him back. For a long time, the county Board of Education didn't want to have anything to do with Scott. They told me our county doesn't have the facilities to educate Scott. They just ignored him. I was really angry. Sending Scott to the school for the deaf was the last resort. I withheld his admission application papers until the very last minute. When the county finally described their proposed program to me, I knew it wouldn't be good for Scott.

"The school for the deaf has helped Scott 100%. Scott was happy as a lark the first semester he went to the state school. He couldn't be any happier. I could see the difference in him. His behavior wasn't as wild. Scott was learning. Scott was so pleased with himself. He's reading now and does math and history. Scott is crazy about science."

"The doctors told me to send George to a school where he would learn to sign. They told me George would always be deaf and would not be able to rely on speech.

"I had to make the decision about which school to put George in. I didn't know anything about deafness. I did what I thought was best. I decided on the state school because it was a continuous program. The children keep going and learning and maybe even go to college. I was impressed when I visited the state school. Seeing all those deaf children running and playing together made me feel better."

"One of the reasons the public schools don't provide special schooling is because the parents don't organize and fight for it. Parents are at fault for not trying to get something done."
(Miki's father)

"I have confidence in the teachers at the school for the deaf. Charlie has had good teachers every year. His teachers have been tuned in to Charlie's needs."

"I didn't want to send the girls away to a residential school. I put them in the county day program to keep them home. They used cued speech at school, and we signed at home. After a few years, I realized they were learning more at home than in school. They just weren't learning enough compared to their abilities. I finally sent them to the state school. Within six weeks I saw 100% improvement. They needed to be with children like themselves and to have friends. There was really a noticeable improvement in what they were learning and in their communication skills. It was hard to send Chrissy away. She was the baby. But it was the best thing to do. All three girls like school."

"I never considered any other schooling besides the school for the deaf. Stacy can't hear."

"We definitely made the right choice to send Eric and Troy to the state school for the deaf. They don't respond to the voice range. Our Board of Education is not prepared to cope with deaf children. They don't have the resources to set up a good program for such a small number of deaf students."

"When we moved back to our home state, we first asked our town about an educational program for Terry. They had nothing.

"Second, we enrolled Terry in our state school for the deaf as a residential student. The third week I was asked to keep Terry home. Terry was not completely toilet trained. (Terry has some delay in motor development.)

"Third, we took Terry to the Rehabilitation Center. They refused to work with Terry because he didn't have any speech.

"Our town finally had to take Terry. Terry was six years old and legally had to be placed in a classroom. And that's what they did. Put him in a classroom.

"I showed Terry's teacher some signs. Then the teacher said her superiors would not permit her to use signs with Terry. I was told to stop signing to Terry at home. I told them I would cooperate everyway to help Terry, but I would not stop signing with him.

"By the end of the school year, the school felt they had made a mistake. Terry was getting behind. They had no experience with deaf children. The teacher and principal realized they had been wrong not to use signs. The teacher admitted she was not the right teacher for Terry. She didn't have any training with deaf children. Her class was for slow learners. For Terry, it had been a wasted year.

"The recommendation was for Terry to return to the state school for the deaf. That summer, I went to our town's Director of Special Education. I just walked in without an appointment and told the director it was important. She listened to me while I told her I wanted a total communication program in town for Terry. Fortunately, P.L. 94-142 came out that summer. Our governor was in favor of the law. Our town knew they could get money for a teacher.

"At first Terry was the only child in the class. Now there are two 14 year olds and two 7 year olds who are deaf. The teacher and aide use total communication. Terry receives individual help with his school work. He can read, add, and subtract. Terry's teacher works him hard.

"Should we keep Terry home in this program or send him back to the state school for the deaf? It's scary not knowing if you are doing the right thing or not. We feel Terry is in a good program now. His teacher cares about him and is concerned about his success."

"I first put Adrienne in an oral school. I wanted her to learn how to attend and to use her residual hearing. I knew Adrienne would eventually go to the state school for the deaf and use signs because she has a profound hearing loss. I didn't think the state school gave enough attention to teaching the children how to listen.

"We started using signs at home while Adrienne was still going to the oral school. The oral school had a real fit.

"Adrienne started going to the state school for the deaf before she was four years old. I'm pleased with the school. I agree with the school's means of teaching and its total communication philosophy. There are small sized classes. More individual attention is provided for the students. I can't see Adrienne in any other program at this point."

"We enrolled Teddy in our county's oral program when he was 18 months old. Teddy saw a speech teacher three times a week for hourly sessions. Teddy was not happy. He didn't like to go. And he really didn't learn much. Teddy was in that program for three years. As far as language growth, those three years were nothing.

"We want Teddy to eventually mainstream with hearing children. We know he is not ready now. So, our preference is for his placement in a self-contained oral classroom. The county is recommending Teddy be placed in their total communication classroom since he has not progressed with the oral approach. But, they don't really use *total* communiction. It's mostly manual communication."

"A deaf child's basic educational needs are for him to attend to his learning and to make progress with academics. Teachers should understand deaf children and these basic needs. Teachers should be deaf themselves or know how to sign. More time should be spent on academics than with speech and hearing activities. We sent Robin to the school for the deaf because we were happy with our experiences and education from deaf schools. Robin is enthusiastic about learning. He wants to know about other countries. He likes to look at maps and globes. Robin asks a lot of questions about history and other people."

"Since our county program puts too much emphasis on teaching speech and auditory training, we sent Saralee to the state school for the deaf. Saralee learns about the world and academics because she understands what is being taught in total communication. Already, she knows about the heart, blood, and what lungs are for. Saralee knows more now than we did when we were her age."

Residential and Day Placement

"I decided to send Kathy Ann to the dorm. She can participate in the activities with the other children. She has the opportunity to learn language easier. Kathy Ann is always ready to go back to school. Sometimes, I still hate to send her back. It's harder on the parents than it is on the kids."

"We don't think Miki is missing that much from home. She's getting so much activity in the dormitory program. Really, it is harder on the parents than the kids. In the very beginning, Miki would scream. We had to be mean and insist that she go back to school. Now, she is always ready."

"Stacy will never go in the dorm. I want her home where she belongs, just like her brothers. They go to school and come home at night. My husband wants his kids home at night. If we didn't live close to the school for the deaf, we would move so Stacy could come home every day."

"We moved to this county so that Robin would have daily transportation to school. We believe it makes our family close to have Robin home. We can give Robin more attention and communication at home than he would receive in the dorm."

"Saralee is too young for the dorm. Her sisters need her at home to play with. We want Saralee home to keep our family close."

"I think children, wherever possible, should stay home, especially if it's not disruptive to the family structure." (Adrienne's mother)

"It was hard to send a four year old away to school. Kevin is the baby in our family. We had never let him out of our sight, not even let him stay over at his grandmother's the way we did with his brothers. It took me about a month to accept it. I still don't like to take him back to school. I can do it because Kevin likes to go. It didn't take him long to get used to school. It's not the same around the house with Kevin gone all week."

"Tim's being away all week was more of an adjustment for us than it was for him. Amy, Tim's sister, still hates Monday mornings. She knows she won't have anyone to play with all week."

"I didn't have the time I wanted to spend with Junior. The school suggested dormitory placement. I make sure I am with Junior every Monday morning so I can see him off. Junior waves and waves. It is so important to him that I see him off to school."

"When Sandy was younger, she used to cry getting on the bus every week. Now, she's ok.

"What's hard is that if Sandy is sick on Sunday and misses the bus, she has to stay home and miss the whole week of school."

"The first year, Eric stayed for after-school activities in the dorm and came home for dinner. The next year, we tried Eric in the dorm full time. Eric cried the first few days. Now, he is happy and always ready to go back to school. We've noticed a big difference in Eric since he has been in the dorm full time. He has learned more signs. And he plays with children better."

"We considered moving closer to the school for the deaf so Tina could be a day student. The difference in the cost of housing is too much for us. Tina has adjusted well to dormitory life. We bring her home for special occasions like our skating party. We always go down to school to see Tina when she is in special programs."

"We kept Stanley in our county total communication program because it was close to home. The bus ride to the state school was too long. We felt we could teach Stanley more at home than he would learn by living in the dormitory at a young age. Next year, when Stanley is six, he will go to the state school and stay in the dorm. The environment at the state school is more of a deaf world. There are more deaf adults and children. Stanley will have the opportunity to have more friends at the school for the deaf."

"We patterned our lives so Stacie and Bobbi Sue could be day students. I have a job which enables me to drive the girls to school every day and gives me the same vacations they have. We are building a home close to the school. Next year, when the house is finished, I will quit my job because the drive will be farther. It's a matter of priorities.

"One year, we had an arrangement where the girls stayed in the dorm for just two nights a week. Now, they stay overnight in the dorm for special occasions. I felt they were safe and well supervised in the dorm when they were younger. I don't feel the supervision is strict enough now."

"No mother and father wants to send their child away. The hardest thing to do is to drop Scott off for the bus and then drive all the way home alone."

"For a long time we thought we should move to the same town where the state school for the deaf is located. We wouldn't have to be away from our boys all week. People in that community know more about deafness and are more accepting. We were told we were selfish not to move. We felt guilty. But this is our home. We grew up here. My husband worked hard to get where he is at work. We talked with other families who did move and were disappointed. We decided not to move. It was a long and difficult decision to make.

"One of my greatest fears was that Eric and Troy wouldn't want to come home after being away so much. It was a bigger adjustment for me. It has taken me five years to accept their being away during the week.
"I think of Eric and Troy every night between 8 and 9. Did they have their bath? Are they happy?
"I used to cry every day. It took me to the middle of the week to get myself together. I realize now I wasted a lot of time. You can just clean your house so many times. Now, I have joined some social clubs and am taking sewing lessons. Sundays are still the worst times. I make a point to have something to do after they leave.

"This is the first year I got myself to accept their being away. They are away. Life goes on. You have to have enough faith that they will be guided through the week.
. . . Every evening I miss Eric and Troy."

"George was the only child here at home. He was very selfish. He always wanted to be first. He would grab things from the other children. George's teacher suggested that he go into the dormitory to be around other children more. It was a good decision."

"Selecting the best school limits where you can live. We are fortunate to have so many programs close by. We let Charlie decide if he wanted to stay in the dormitory. Charlie was a day student for a year and a half. Then I tried to encourage his trying the dorm. There are no children in our neighborhood for him to play with, and the dormitory program offers well-planned activities. Charlie's sister, Holly, was taking on too much responsibility with Charlie at home. "Charlie has been a dorm student for two and a half years. Right now, I feel depressed when I pack his suitcase Sunday nights. Charlie has started to have problems in the dorm. I will do anything to make Charlie happy. I was ready to pull him out of the dorm. We talked our concerns over with the school. The older boys are too rough with the younger boys. Charlie was learning dirty signs from the older kids. The deaf dormitory counselors use Ameslan while at school and at home Charlie uses signed English.

"We have adjusted our personal lives to Charlie as a dorm student. We both work. And Holly has changed. She accepts all the attention Charlie receives on the weekend because she knows she gets attention during the week when Charlie is at school. I'm not sure about next year. We'll see how the rest of this year goes."

"We both went to residential school. Edna's older sister and brother live in the dormitory. Edna's friends stay in the dorm. Edna was tired of the long bus ride every day. So Edna is a dormitory student."

School and Family Working Together

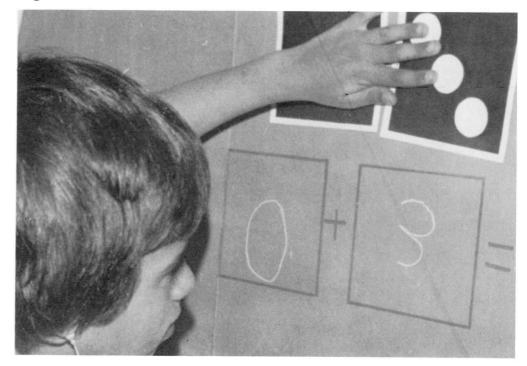

"The school for the deaf is good for Junior. But the family will have to help him learn. He can't get it all in school. We will have to help him."

"Our home is a signed English, total communication environment. We selected the school for Roger and Tom that would reinforce this philosophy."

"I am aware of what Adrienne is learning in her classroom. I try to do follow up activities to make her school work more meaningful. We took a train ride when she was studying transportation."

"Saralee was put ahead one class. It was hard for her the first month. But we helped her with her school work and encouraged her every day at home. Now, Saralee is happy and very successful in this class."

"I go over the school work Billy brings home everyday. His teachers and I communicate in a book that Billy carries to and from school."

"I help Julie and Kristy with their homework. And I go over with them all the school work they bring home."

8

Deaf Awareness and Further Acceptance

The deaf child and his parents become teachers of deaf awareness. Through their actions, parents demonstrate their understanding of deafness and their attitude toward deafness to:
- —their deaf children
- —their immediate families
- —their extended families
- —their neighbors
- —their communities.

Awareness and understanding of deafness is not common knowledge in our society. Hearing parents who are suddenly forced to become aware and to learn about deafness frequently find it difficult to deal with the ignorance and misconceptions of their families and friends.

Deaf Awareness and Acceptance: The Deaf Child's Self Concept

"Teddy kicked a girl who was staring at him. He knows something is different."

"When Stanley was around four years old, he said, 'me deaf,' pointed to his ears, and said, 'no.'"

"Once when we saw some hearing children, Tina asked if they sign or talk. Then she said, 'I don't talk. I like to sign better.' Since her brother Tony was born, Tina has been very interested to know if he will talk and if he will go to her school."

"Billy has always had a sense that he was different. When he comes home from school and sees that someone is visiting, he takes his hearing aid off before he comes in the door. This is the first year Billy left his hearing aid on for his school picture. I've tried to talk with him about his being deaf and to tell him that the other kids will like him anyway. So far, Billy has refused to talk about it. One time we saw another family signing to each other. Billy said he was the same as that boy and went over to talk with him."

"Stacy wears her hearing aid very little at home. She knows she is different from the other kids, so she won't wear it. On school days, her hearing aid is the first thing she puts on in the morning."

"As soon as Eric gets in the car to come home from school, he takes his hearing aid off. Maybe he feels embarrassed that no one else in the family wears one."

"When Charlie was little he thought everyone knew how to sign. He would go up to anyone and sign to them. When he was seven, Charlie realized he was deaf and not everyone else is deaf, too. He has become very self-conscious. When we go out to a restaurant, Charlie doesn't want anyone to see him sign. He refuses to wear his hearing aid. The first thing he wants to know about new people he meets is if they are deaf or hearing. Sometimes, Charlie gets in a somber mood and tells us how bad he feels about being the only deaf person in the family. He asks for a deaf brother."

Deaf Awareness and Acceptance: Brothers and Sisters

"My son Kenny helps my husband when Stacy uses a sign he doesn't know."

"Tina doesn't always understand the extra time I spend with Billy. She really is more understanding than I would expect. Billy gets along well with Tina. They sign to each other."

"Stacie was happy when she found out Bobbi Sue was deaf, too. She got her old hearing aid out to give to her."

"Tim and Amy are very close. Sometimes Amy is motherly towards Tim. Sometimes she is jealous. She asks why I spend more time with Timmy. Amy wishes she were deaf so she could get the extra attention."

"Charlie feels more comfortable around hearing people when his (hearing) sister Holly is with him. Sometimes we worry that we are giving Holly too much responsibility. Charlie really depends on her."

"Randy feels sorry for Teddy and gives into him more easily. Teddy's older brother John makes sure Teddy gets a fair deal when they are playing outside with the neighborhood kids."

Deaf Awareness and Acceptance: The Extended Family

"My parents still ask, 'Are you sure Teddy's deaf?' They talk in long sentences. They just don't understand."

"My parents' not wanting to learn to sign has hurt me. I have bitter feelings about their lack of concern for their grandson. The rift between Charlie and them was predictable. You can't be close to someone with whom you can't communicate. They look at Charlie and grin at him. In my opinion, it is their fault. It doesn't take much time to learn just the alphabet. My parents have convinced themselves not to make the effort. Charlie initiates communication with them. He writes them little notes. He takes the sign dictionary with him when he visits and points to the words he wants to tell them. Charlie is not inhibited by the communication barrier, yet. He loves them."

"My sisters still won't learn to sign. . . . A hug just isn't enough."
(Billy's mother)

"Billy's grandfather calls me up and tells me how sorry he is. I don't want to hear sympathy. I can't get him to come and visit the school for the deaf and see all that the deaf children do."

"We bought sign books for our relatives last Christmas. They are starting to become interested in signing with Tina. They are recognizing what Tina is signing to them. I think they sign more with Tina when we are out of the room because they are still a little embarrassed."

"My mother thinks there ought to be some kind of an operation that will make Sandy hear."

"We usually end up interpreting for Bobbi Sue and Stacie when we are with our relatives. I expected my family to learn to sign. I tried to teach them. I don't feel like I am close to my family because of the communication problem. It's more than a communication problem. Some of my family feel uneasy, uncomfortable around the girls. They don't understand deafness. When you can't communicate, there is an obstacle that makes you feel uncomfortable."

"None of my relatives accept my deaf children. They won't learn to sign. They don't visit anymore. My family is drifting apart. This hurts."
(Troy and Eric's mother)

"Because deafness was already in the family, everyone readily accepted Tim."

"My relatives treat Sandy like an infant."

"My family has been supportive, interested, and concerned. Sometimes they are a little over-protective."
(Adrienne's mother)

"My mom won't accept Kathy Ann's deafness. She expects Kathy Ann to hear again all of a sudden. She doesn't understand the signs, so she isn't going to use them."

"Most of my family has taken sign classes. My younger sister has become a teacher of the deaf."
(Tom and Roger's mother)

"I can accept annoying statements from strangers, but when they come from my family, it hurts my feelings."
(Terry's mother)

Deaf Awareness and Acceptance: Hearing Peers

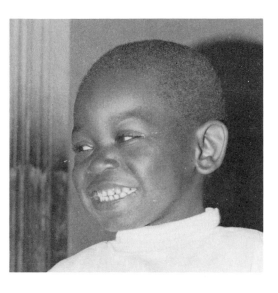

"Kathy Ann learns from playing with the other kids and by copying them."

"Sending Eric to Head Start with hearing children helped him. He learned to be more independent and to play better."

"Teddy enjoyed joining in the different activities at his hearing nursery school."

"Charlie is lonely. In our old neighborhood none of the kids would play with him because we insisted he stay in the yard. Since we have moved, there are no children here for him to play with."

"In our old neighborhood, Roger and Tom were left out of the games the kids played. I tried to entice the kids over. They were really nice kids, but, for the most part, they didn't have the patience. The girls came over and tried to mother the boys, but the boys couldn't be bothered with them. When a hearing kid is in a one-to-one situation with a deaf kid, it's all right. But, as soon as there are two hearing kids, the deaf kid gets left out. We do more as a family because of this."

"We taught signs to the neighborhood children so Stacie and Bobbi Sue would feel more comfortable around them."

"The neighborhood kids tease Junior. They laugh at him and make fun of the noises he makes when he talks. Junior comes in the house crying."

"In our old neighborhood the kids made fun of Eric. I talked to their parents and asked them how they would like it if someone made fun of their kid. I didn't have any more trouble after that."

"Terry tries to mix right in with the other children at the playground. Most of the kids don't make fun of him. They seem interested in Terry. When they see me using signs with him, they ask me what the signs mean and to teach them some signs. They try to communicate with Terry. Sometimes the older girls try to mother Terry. I explain to them that Terry must learn to be independent. I think it's good for Terry to get out and be with the other kids."

"Stacy is around hearing people all the time. Many of the neighborhood children and cousins know signs from being around the house. Those that don't know signs ask me what Stacy is saying."

"Because there is more deaf awareness today, some of the neighborhood kids have learned fingerspelling and some signs at their public school. And Eric and Troy teach their friends some signs."

Deaf Awareness and Acceptance: The General Public

"It's still awkward out in public, when people stare, when they start to talk to Charlie. People over-react and get embarrassed when we tell them Charlie is deaf, and then we get embarrassed. I usually just answer for Charlie and move on to avoid the embarrassment. Sometimes, I feel like going up and telling people they should know better than to stare, but I usually just ignore them."

"When people say, 'Those girls are deaf and dumb,' I tell them the proper term is deaf and mute, and that mute is not accurate either. Bobbi and Stacie can talk."

"Some people are really insensitive. Sometimes mothers pull their children away from Terry. I continue to take Terry out and let people know he is deaf. People are going to learn to get used to deafness. People have to stop hiding it. We have to teach people that deaf children belong in the mainstream of life and not hidden away in institutions. A disease can cause a hearing loss; a hearing loss is not a disease."

"I am proud to sign in public with my family to teach hearing people that this is the way we communicate."
(Edna's mother)

"So many people see Adrienne's deafness before they see Adrienne the child. "Many people, when they see her, want to say something, but don't know what to say. Stupid statements come out like, 'Too bad she has to wear those things (hearing aids).' Often, I have to grit my teeth because I know they don't mean it.
"When the problem was thrust upon me so suddenly, I had to do a lot of self-educating about deafness. Then I tried to answer all the questions people put to me. I found most people know very little, know nothing, or have misconceptions about deafness.
"Society and the media have done a terrific job making deafness more visible. I see so many more things designed for all handicapped people in general. All that has helped. I don't see or hear as many dumb statements anymore . . . Maybe I'm just not as sensitive to them as I was previously."

"There is more public awareness about deafness today. My relatives are always pointing out articles and TV programs about deafness to me. Five years ago, that wasn't the case." (Tim's mother)

"The park where Chrissy plays has a summer program that includes the deaf children in with the hearing children. The counselor is deaf."

"When people ask dumb questions like, 'Is her hearing getting better?', I tell them straight out I think it embarrasses the child when they say things like that." (Julie's mother)

"Usually when people ask about my children, and I tell them they are both deaf, they react with sympathy." (Robin's mother)

"People around here expect Julie and Kristy to hear and talk when they put their hearing aids on."

"Other people worry about Stacy's deafness more than I do. They ask me if I tried acupuncture. They act like they don't think I'm trying to help her."

"What annoys me is that other people keep expecting Teddy to hear with his hearing aid or by some kind of miracle. It really annoys me when people clap their hands behind him to see if he will respond.
"Teddy probably knows how to handle people better than they know how to deal with him."

"Where I work, people know I have a deaf son. They watch out for any news about deafness and tell me." (Charlie's mother)

"Now that our church has started to interpret the services, Tim doesn't fuss about going to church. Before, he really didn't like to go and just sit."

9

Multihandicapped Hearing Impaired Children

Multihandicapped hearing impaired children are those hearing impaired children who have additional handicapping conditions which require special education beyond the education prescribed for their hearing loss. The handicaps that are present in a population of normally hearing children can also be found among deaf children. These additional handicaps include: mental retardation, emotional disturbances, physical disabilities, language impairments, specific learning disabilities, and/or visual handicaps.

A problem faced by parents of multihandicapped deaf children is in finding an appropriate educational setting. Most special education programs are prepared to work with only one kind of handicapping condition resulting in the exclusion of the child with multi-handicaps. For example, the child who is deaf-emotionally disturbed is excluded from the educational program for deaf children because of his emotional problems. And he is excluded from the educational program for emotionally disturbed children because he is deaf.

It is sometimes difficult to accurately measure a multihandicapped child's hearing. Children having brain damage or an emotional disturbance may not respond to sounds or speech even though their peripheral auditory systems are intact.

Kenny

"Before Kenny was two years old, I felt something was wrong. He wasn't talking. The doctor said to wait; some children are slow to talk. We finally went to a clinic, several trips there, then to the Child Development Center, back to the pediatrician, to a psychologist, and then to the school for the deaf. It has been a miserable run-a-round. We got so many conflicting opinions. We didn't know what to believe.

"I know Kenny's not mentally retarded. He can put puzzles together after he's had the chance to work with them. I've visited the state program for the mentally retarded, and I don't feel Kenny acts like the people there. My pediatrician advised against placing Kenny in that program. He felt it would be a bad environment for Kenny. Who can tell me what Kenny's problem is and what I can do to help him?

"All these diagnoses are expensive. One trip for an EEG was $50. Because Kenny didn't respond to the sedative, he didn't have the test. The second trip for the same test cost $85. Just that one test cost $135, and we still didn't get any answers."

Kenny's Age	Professional Services	Diagnoses, Referrals, Programs
15 mo.	pediatrician	Kenny's delay in talking could be normal. Wait.
2	pediatrician	Kenny might be deaf. We were referred to an audiologist and an Ear-Nose-Throat doctor.
2½	audiologist	A hearing evaluation could not be obtained.
	ENT doctor	Nothing was found to be wrong.
	child psychiatrist	Kenny was diagnosed as retarded.
	pediatrician	We were referred to the school for the deaf.

"I feel there is something wrong beyond the hearing problem. Kenny doesn't try to communicate. He's never even pointed. He doesn't pay attention. The discipline is so hard, correcting him over and over again for the same things. I have to watch Kenny constantly. He's gone into water over his head. He's drunk gasoline.

"The dentist was nasty. I told him Kenny had a special problem. He said everybody has problems. We did find a barber who was patient. He took the time to show Kenny the clippers, etc.

"I just take one day at a time. That's all I can do."

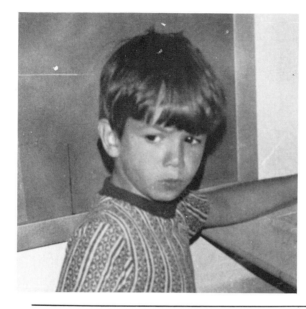

Kenny's Age	Professional Services	Diagnoses, Referrals, Programs
3	audiologist	A test could not be achieved. Kenny was referred to the pre-school program for deaf children.
3-4	state school for the deaf preschool parent counseling program	Teachers visited us at home on a weekly basis. This was a total communication program.
4	audiologist	Some sensitivity for hearing was found. A complete hearing test was not achieved.
	psychologist	Kenny was diagnosed as having additional handicaps beyond the hearing loss.
	hospital	An EEG found no cerebral damage.

"The program for multi-handicapped deaf children was good except we didn't like Kenny's being away from home during the week. Since we didn't know how long he would stay in this program, we decided not to sell our house and move closer.

"Kenny had his first seizure when he was six years old. His seizures are very serious and have required hospitalization. It was even harder to leave Kenny in a residential school knowing he might have another seizure and we wouldn't be there."

Kenny's Age	Professional Services	Diagnoses, Referrals, Programs
4-7	state school for the deaf program for multihandicapped hearing impaired children	Kenny was a residential student in this program that used total communication and behavior modification in the school and dorm. Kenny learned to respond for a hearing evaluation by practicing in continuous and structured training sessions.
6	audiologist	A valid hearing test was obtained that showed Kenny to have normal hearing. Kenny was referred back to our county for a more appropriate educational setting.

"We are careful not to expect too much from professionals. We just expect the worse. Then, if nothing happens, we are prepared. If something does come of the visit, we are pleasantly surprised.

"Professionals give us recommendations and then send us back home.

"Anyone with an opinion is an expert.

"We really have not received any encouragement from a professional.

"The counseling experts don't help. We need practical help, a break during the day, financial help. It's no help to pay a babysitter and then drive just to hear someone talk for a half an hour about a situation he doesn't understand.

"Kenny is not normal. Mentally retarded refers to anyone who does not function at a normal level. It didn't surprise me. When Kenny started school, I realized. But you hope, cry, pray.

"You always hope for a magic cure. I agree with his teachers who see evidence of memory, intelligence, and reason. There's that desire to find the key to unlock his intelligence. Kenny is like a car out of tune. We just haven't found the right adjustment, yet.

"I really don't know any more today than I knew when Kenny was two years old."

Kenny's Age	Professional Services	Diagnoses, Referrals, Programs
6	pupil placement counselor	The county requested an intense and complete evaluation prior to educational placement.
	evaluation team: • specialist in language learning disabilities • audiologist • psychologist • psychiatrist • neurologist • pediatrician • sociologist	This team found Kenny: to have a severe language disorder to have inappropriate adaptive social behavior to be multihandicapped to be unique not to be functioning at his chronological age

"Kenny understands what we say to him with our voice alone. He signs and uses his voice, points, pulls us to what he wants, or gets it himself. No one can understand his speech but us. I doubt he will ever have intelligible speech. We think now that he is in a school with speaking peers, Kenny is more motivated to use his voice.

"We are probably both guilty of expecting too little from Kenny. We should be more strict. It's for our convenience that we're not.

"Now that Kenny is getting older, his handicaps are more noticeable. The symptoms are more pronounced, more obvious. Taking medicine to control his seizures has caused a weight gain. People prefer to play with Kenny's younger brother because he is still cute. I feel sorry for Kenny.

"Kenny is in a good educational program. He is happy. He likes getting on the school bus every morning. Kenny gets a lot of individualized instruction. His teachers understand his signs. Kenny tries so hard."

"I don't know where Kenny will be next year or two years from now.

"As you live through the situation, you become immune to it. I couldn't imagine my life any other way now. You couldn't do it alone. We just take one day at a time."

Kenny's Age	Professional Services	Diagnoses, Referrals, Programs
7-8	county special education program	Kenny has been attending school as a day student. He receives classroom instruction, language therapy, and motor therapy.

Teddy

"Teddy definitely was a high risk child. No one really knew what was wrong. It seems to have been a delay in his motor development. "We waited it out and worked with Teddy as we did with our other children. Teddy was delayed in toilet training and walking. For a long time, he was clumsy, always falling. He just matured.

"Now, everything has caught up. Teddy runs, jumps, skips, and rides his bike. Teddy doesn't need special education for more than his hearing loss."

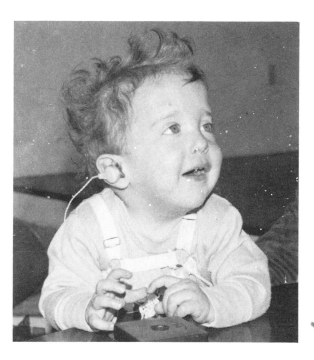

10

Hard of Hearing Children

Hard of hearing children are those children with a hearing loss who can, to some degree, discriminate speech sounds and understand speech through the use of their hearing. Hard of hearing children need support and training to fully acquire language and to produce speech.

Hard of hearing children are not deaf, and they are not hearing. They have a specific set of communicational, social, and educational needs. Because the number of hard of hearing children in one area is so few, it is frequently difficult to find an educational program designed for them.

Communication

"A lot of people think Danny can hear better than he does because he talks so much. I have to explain to them that you don't know how much he is hearing. Danny doesn't hear whole conversations. He gets only bits and pieces. Danny is not grasping everything. We have to scream at him when he's not wearing his hearing aid. Discipline is difficult. It takes longer to get through to him. Danny's language is confused. He can't explain things. He gets his stories mixed up. He doesn't have an understanding of time. He starts a story and then jumps to events from past years and then to something that has happened a month or two ago."

"Tom is hard of hearing. His brother Roger is deaf. Because Roger is deaf, we decided to make our home a total communication environment. We wanted Tom and Roger to be able to communicate and grow together. Through the use of total communication and signed English, Tom has internalized the basic English language structure. He understands his father's speech now without the need for signs. I use signs and talk a little louder to Tom. Tom and Roger usually communicate orally with each other. When they are not understanding, they add manual communication. We let them decide their means to communicate. Tom successfully uses his speech with the neighborhood kids and our relatives. I still interpret TV shows for him. The talking on them is usually too fast for him to follow."

"Sometimes Paul hears words, but he doesn't comprehend them. He knows he is being spoken to, but he doesn't understand the full sentence. There are certain letter combinations he doesn't hear. I get really angry when people who have observed this tell me Paul is only hearing what he wants to hear.

"Paul's biggest problem is hearing his playmates. Some of his friends just don't talk loud enough. They don't mind repeating for Paul.

"I sometimes feel I have to be close by to explain things to Paul. At baseball practice, for example, the other kids get the directions so much faster. I stay close by to make it easier for Paul.

"We have always made the effort to talk with Paul and to have conversations with him. I have always stopped and attended whenever Paul talked to me. I tried my best to understand what he was saying. I have always responded to Paul's communication.

"We used signs with Paul for about a year or more, until he started talking. Paul stopped using signs when he no longer needed them.

"We always had signs to fall back on when the need arose, when he had an ear infection or if I wasn't understanding him. I don't regret having used signs. They helped Paul realize all things had names. And Paul was always able to express himself. Paul is proof that signs don't slow down speech development. Everything is verbal now. Paul's speech is very good. There are still some words he doesn't pronounce correctly. If I can't understand a word, I ask Paul to explain more about it. Paul is not inhibited about talking. No one seems to notice his speech as being different."

Education

"We chose to start Tom at the school for the deaf because it used the same signed English, total communication philosophy we use at home. And, we didn't feel Tom had enough hearing to succeed in public school. We thought the kids at public school would tease Tom. Kids always pick on the kid who is different. We didn't want Tom to be unhappy and frustrated in school. Tom is happy at the school for the deaf. He has succeeded socially as well as academically.

"This past year we tried mainstreaming Tom in our neighborhood public school. We felt Tom needed more exposure to hearing people and that he could handle more academics. Tom no longer needs the class time spent on communication skills and language development which he has been receiving at the school for the deaf.

"Tom's homeroom teacher was very willing to have him. Tom was tested and accepted academically at his grade level. While he was in this school, Tom moved up to a higher math and reading level. Tom received speech therapy twice a week.

"After four months, we returned Tom to the school for the deaf. He was just missing too much. We went in and observed him through a whole school day. Mainstreaming did not work for Tom in this situation because the school was an open classroom environment, Tom had to mainstream the whole school day all at once, and he was alone in trying this. Because of the open environment, the children and teachers whispered to keep the noise level down. One of his teachers talked fast and with his back turned. Tom missed lessons when records were used. Tom was frustrated because he didn't understand the rules at recess.

"Tom was enthusiastic about going to public school. He was on the school basketball team. He made some friends whom he still plays ball with and sees at birthday parties. But, when he cried so hard after trying his best, we decided to send him back to the school for the deaf. We explained to Tom that he did not fail and that maybe he could try again.

"Tom finished this school year at the school for the deaf. Since he is academically ahead of his deaf peers by two years, he was in a class with older kids. Tom socializes well with his older deaf classmates."

"I believe Danny needs special education. After six years of school, Danny is functioning academically between a first and second year level for math and reading. This last school year Danny made a gain of four months progress. Danny does not like school. He is not happy. His attitude toward school is becoming more and more negative. He is stubborn and rebellious about school and homework.

"When he first started at our neighborhood school, the kids called Danny 're-tarded.' I tried to explain to him that he was going to the resource room for help with his school work because of his hearing problem.

"Next year, the school is planning to push him on to fourth grade. I am requesting a three month trial period because I have not been pleased with his academic progress or his behavior. There is no alternative to fourth grade placement except to retain him in the third grade. How will Danny be able to cope next year in fourth grade when he found it so hard this year?"

Danny's Age	Educational Program
4	Our county school superintendent sent us to the state school for the deaf. Danny was not accepted because he has too much hearing. Our county school superintendent told us of a program for hearing impaired children in a neighboring county. I had no way of sending Danny until I found another parent willing to drive him.
5	Our county sent Danny to a special program in a second neighboring county.
6	Danny was mainstreamed into a first grade class through this county's program.
7	Danny was sent to a special class in a large town in our county.
8	Danny was mainstreamed into a second grade class through this town's program.
9	Danny was mainstreamed into a third grade class at our neighborhood school with two hours a day spent in a resource room for academic work.

"I believe in summer school for kids. Paul has always gone to summer school. It helps him keep up with what he has learned through the school year. Paul likes to go to summer school.

"It has not been easy finding a good educational program for Paul. Either he had too much hearing or not enough. But, I never quit looking, asking, and pushing for the best education for my son. I have always watched Paul's progress closely and will continue to do so. I will keep fighting for Paul.

"I have been especially concerned with Paul's learning to read. We have encouraged Paul to read by reading together. Before Paul could read, I read stories to him. Paul reads to his father while riding in the dump truck. We play reading games, like, I read Paul a page, then he reads me a page. Paul picks out words he knows in the newspaper.

Last summer, we paid Paul for every book he read. Paul read 37 books. It resulted in his skipping a whole reader when he went back to school. I ask Paul questions about the books to check on his comprehension. Paul understands what he reads. He enjoys reading and often chooses to read on his own."

Paul's Age	Educational Program
3	Paul attended a hearing nursery school. Paul started private speech therapy.

4,5	I did not want Paul to attend our city's program for hearing impaired children.
	    The speech services were poor.
	    Placement was with mentally retarded children.
	    Transportation required a long bus ride.
	I put Paul in a private hearing school.
	Paul continued with private speech therapy.

5½	After investigating different educational programs for Paul, we moved to a county which, I felt, had the best to offer. Paul attended our new neighborhood school until he could be evaluated and recommended for the special hearing impaired program. I had to push for this evaluation to be completed. Paul continued with private speech therapy.

Paul's Age	Educational Program
6,7	For two years, Paul attended an excellent special class for hearing impaired and language disabled children. There were one teacher and two aides for the eight children in Paul's class. The teacher was trained in speech and language development. Paul received speech therapy in school four times a week for half hour sessions.
8	Paul attended a Minimal Learning Disabilities Class. The goal of this class is to mainstream the children into their regular grade level class which is based in the same school. Paul was integrated into third grade for P.E., lunch, recess, and art. His MLD class was small with only ten children. Paul's teacher identified his needs and worked on preparing him for mainstreaming. Paul learned phonics this year which helped his spelling and reading. Paul's reading scores doubled. He is reading on grade level. His vocabulary scores are above grade level. Paul learned to independently complete his homework. Paul received speech therapy. Next year Paul is scheduled to increase his mainstreaming to include math and reading in the fourth grade class.

Social Development

"Tom is at a real disadvantage. He doesn't fit in the hearing world or the deaf world. He is really stuck in the middle. It's not going to be easy for him to be accepted by either group. Right now, Tom needs exposure to both. We are helping him to have the ability to communicate so he can feel at ease with either group. Then, Tom can decide if he wants to be part of the deaf world, the hearing world, or both.

"Tom knows he is hard of hearing and Roger is deaf. He corrects anyone who says they are both deaf.

"Tom and Roger have always been close. Roger teachers Tom what he learns at school, the alphabet, to read maps, etc. Even though they are close, they are different. Roger chooses to stay in the dorm during the week. Tom prefers to come home every day and play with the neighborhood kids."

"When Danny was younger, I kept him in the house more than our other children. He had to be constantly watched because he was always getting into things. I couldn't always watch him, and it wasn't fair to expect his brothers to watch him. I still insist that Danny stay in our yard. He is starting to rebel and run off when I'm not watching.

"Danny doesn't get along with his brothers. They are aware of his hearing loss, but they don't accept it. They fight with Danny because he can't hear them. They call him names, 'retarded,' 'dumb little moron.' The names hurt Danny. He gets back at them by tattling on them.

"We go to Church every Sunday. Danny made his First Communion, but he doesn't really understand.

"Three of our children have handicaps. I am more tolerant with my handicapped children when they misbehave because of their problems."
(Danny's father)

"We do a lot of things together as a family. There are few places we go or things we do that Paul doesn't join us. Paul helped us dig the yard for our swimming pool. We go bowling together. We have family cook-outs. Paul really likes to work and help around the house. He takes the trash out and clears the dishes from the table. Friday is his night to cook. Paul loves to clean his dad's dump truck, wash it and vacuum the inside.

"Paul's first love is playing with his toy trucks. He also plays the guitar and organ, likes to read books and write letters, plays baseball, swims, and rides his bike.

"Paul likes to independently go in and give our order at McDonald's. When he first tried this, we got two of everything because he repeated the order to make sure the girl understood him.

"When Paul was younger, he would ask why other people didn't wear hearing aids. He's pretty comfortable with his hearing loss. He teases his cousin and tells him, 'You know I don't understand you when you mumble. Open your mouth and talk right.'

"We haven't allowed Paul to take advantage of his hearing loss. He has to live in this world. We don't want him to be obnoxious."

Appendix

The 29 families who participated in this study were taken from the rolls of the Maryland School for the Deaf Preschool Parent Counseling Program in April of 1974. This program is open to all families in the State of Maryland who have preschool aged children believed to have a hearing loss. The Maryland School for the Deaf (M.S.D.) is a total communication school; thus, it attracts a biased sample with regard to communication philosophy.

The participants of this study learned about the M.S.D. Program either by contacting the school independently or by referral of their audiological clinic, county health department, county department of education, or pediatrician.

When the study began, the average age of the children was 3.5 years. The distribution of their ages was:

age	percent	number
0-1	3%	1
1-2	10%	3
2-3	14%	4
3-4	38%	11
4-5	31%	9
5-6	3%	1

The most frequent cause of the children's hearing loss was a genetic cause. The cause is defined as genetic when there is another member of the family with a hearing loss. Both parents are deaf in four of the families. The distribution of etiologies is:

cause	percent	number
genetic	41%	12
unknown	31%	9
meningitis	21%	6
birth complication	7%	2

There are two multihandicapped hearing impaired children in the group.

Most of the children have a severe to profound hearing loss. The following distribution of hearing losses is based on valid responses to pure-tone audiometric testing which was achieved by April 1978:

intensity at which child responded to pure tones	description of hearing loss	percent	number
0-25 dB.	normal hearing	3%	1
26-40 dB.	mild	0%	0
41-55 dB.	moderate	7%	2
56-70 dB.	moderately-severe	7%	2
71-90 dB.	severe	21%	6
91 dB.	profound	62%	18

General interviews were conducted in the spring of 1974. Four years later the families were again interviewed using a prepared list of questions based on the concerns they had initially expressed.

Photographs were taken in homes and school programs in 1974 and 1978.